Shattered

Dreams

Losing a Child to Suicide & Surviving
30 Years of Abuse

Comfort Addy

About the Author

Comfort is an African-Canadian mother, survivor, and advocate who endured almost 30 years in a marriage defined by control, emotional, physical abuse, financial manipulation, and deep psychological trauma. Her life has been shaped by unimaginable hardship, including the devastating loss of her beloved Son, Addy, a respectful, brilliant, and compassionate man, almost 25 years old, who died by suicide after years of enduring relentless abuse and unresolved PTSD he suffered at the hands of his own biological father.

A woman of deep resilience and quiet strength. Comfort stayed in her marriage far too long, out of fear, cultural expectations, feeling ashamed, and a desperate hope to protect her children. But silence, she came to realize, can cost more than anyone should ever have to pay.

Addy's death, and the tragic aftermath that followed, including further violence inflicted on others by her former spouse, awakened a fire in her: a need to speak out, not just for herself, but for every mother, child, and survivor who has suffered in silence.

Today, Comfort uses her voice to break the generational cycle of abuses, the generational silence on various subjects that matter to society, such as the Landlord and Tenant Ordeal. Check out her book on the subject on Amazon titled: "The Trials & Tribulations Of Landlords Against Professional Tenants." She also uses her voice to advocate for mental health awareness, especially within immigrant and African communities where stigma and silence often prevail. Through writing, public speaking, and outreach, she channels her grief into purpose, honoring her Son's memory by refusing to let his story be forgotten.

This memoir is her offering to the world: a tribute to Addy, a testament of survival, and a powerful reminder that even after great loss, healing is possible and necessary.

Dedication

This book is dedicated to my beloved son, Addy, a brilliant, caring, and dedicated soul who was stolen from this world too soon. At just 24, Addy left this world, heartbroken beyond belief. He was a 6'2 young man full of promises that battled PTSD and scars left on him by a father who chose control over compassion. Addy was the light in my life, his siblings, and close friends. His life was extinguished too soon. This is my story of pain, survival, and hope for others living in the shadows. My Son was such a bright light that was cut down by the very patriarch who was supposed to protect him. His laughter, intelligence, caring, empathy, and respectfulness inspired everyone around him. This is not just my story, it's his. It's a tribute to his resilience and a wake-up call to those trapped in the darkness of living in abusive homes.

This book is meant to help others and exhibit that through heartbreak and survival, this memoir must shine a spotlight on the hidden causes of domestic abuse and the profound impact it has on the ones we love most.

Acknowledgment

Special thanks to my publisher, McGilligan Publishing Group, for their help, support, and guidance in writing this heartfelt book to help others live a meaningful life without abuse.

Their expertise and dedication have been insurmountable throughout this journey. Starting from redefining my ideas to shaping them into a softer narrative, their insight and encouragement have made all the difference.

Thank you greatly for believing in this project and for helping me navigate the complexities of publishing with professionalism and care. This book would not have come to life without all your efforts in sharing this compelling story with the world. I'm immensely grateful for your unwavering role in making this vision a reality. Thank you, Daniel White, Emma Parker, Priscilla Tessa, and others not mentioned.

Contents

Introduction

For almost thirty years, I lived in a cage built by fear, deception, and violence. This is the story of how I endured and ultimately escaped a life of abuse with a man who drained the life out of our family, stole my children's future, and destroyed our lives in ways no one could have ever imagined. It's a tale of survival against all odds, and a reminder that even in the darkest of times, there is HOPE...

Chapter 1: The Beginning

I grew up modestly in a Christian household, being the first of seven children in a humble family that was respectful, and was brought up in a strict manner to work hard in order to survive in life. I did well in school and loved to study. I competed hard to get the best grade, and life was okay.

I finished high school, and where I hailed from, college wasn't optional. So off I went, on a faithful day in the late 80s, to go and attend an interview for admission into college.

On getting there, I met several prospective student battling to be admitted as well, so there were lots of talks, laughter, jokes, and nonchalant attitudes on some, while some had fear, anxiety, and desperation in their demeanours, and were not sure whether they'll get admission into the school or not.

That was how we first crossed paths during this particular college interview. I was one of those with an anxious demeanour while my ex was the faction with the nonchalant attitudes and joker expressions. I wish the universe had warned me right there that this is not someone to get close to, but as the day went on, I started feeling uneasy around him. I confronted him that he wasn't serious and too loud, not knowing it was my intuition and the universe that was warning me that he was a troubled human being.

As said earlier, he was loud, somehow funny, yet obnoxious. After I called him out on his behaviour, we ended up becoming friends after being accepted into the same department.

When school started, I later found out that he was a skilled storyteller. He often shared tales about how he grew up and single-handedly supported his entire family. His stories moved me, and I started wondering if a guy could do so much for his siblings and mother, then what he wouldn't do for his own immediate family one day.

We were friends for a long time, and nothing more than that. However, as time went on, this man kept telling me more and more stories about his family. He started making me feel sorry for him, sometimes crying while telling me these tales. I was so naïve, and I'll say gullible, for falling for all those cooked-up stories until I was completely engulfed in his web of lies. There were signs, subtle hints that he might not be telling the truth, but because he kept up with these tales perfectly, I began to believe them, and then the love affair started without me realizing it.

How we started dating still baffles me. He wasn't the type I'd typically go for. I've always had a softer spot for tall guys; he's short. I always had a flair for light-skinned guys; he's darker in tone. I always wanted a guy who is intelligent, and he was as dumb as a rock, but intelligent enough to mask his lack of intelligence with jokes and dramas. He was smooth with every behavior, heavily calculated. The abuse started subtly, creeping in like shadows in the night, and I did not realize it.

After moving in with him post-college, it did not take long before the abuse started. It started with quick dismissals of my opinions, often ridiculing me in front of the others in a way that seemed like harmless teasing. Yet, beneath the surface, I could feel a growing unease. I chose to ignore all the comments and subtle disrespects, believing that patience and ignoring him would smooth over the rough edges, but the more I ignored, the more he kept with the abuses and diminishing my state of mind, kept piling the blame on me.

Chapter 2: The Mask Slips

As time passed, the man I thought I knew, the man who portrayed himself as the caretaker of all his siblings and mother, began to change. Or perhaps, more accurately, his true nature started to emerge. His laziness started showing, refusing to work hard or take any responsibility for our growing family. The burden of providing for our children fell entirely on my shoulders. I worked tirelessly to make ends meet, all while enduring his constant complaints, demands, and countless abuses.

He began isolating me from friends and family, ensuring that his control over me tightened with each passing day. I felt alone, trapped in a marriage that was becoming increasingly suffocating. The charming man I thought I met in college was gone, replaced by someone cold, manipulative, and violent towards me and the kids. He's calculated in every way, always putting on a brave face, making everyone believe that he has a perfect family with a perfect wife and kids.

We became the envy of our friends and families, who believed that our family was the epitome of happiness that every family must copy. However, they didn't realize what was going on behind our closed door, that the man they were envying is two-faced, that he has countless women outside with tons of kids outside the marriage, unbeknownst to me at home.

Chapter 3: The Abuser Revealed

As he was busy polishing his image to the outside world, so was he busy multitasking, raining his terror on me and the kids inside the house. The first time he hit me, I was in shock. I had seen flashes of his temper, but I never imagined it would escalate to physical violence. I convinced myself it was a one-time incident, an outburst that wouldn't happen again. But I was wrong. The abuse became more frequent, and with each act of violence, a part of me withered away.

I learned to walk on eggshells, always trying to avoid anything that might trigger his rage. But no matter what I did, it was never enough. The abuse took many forms: verbal, emotional, and physical. He demeaned me, made me feel worthless, and slowly eroded any sense of self-worth I had left.

Chapter 4: A House of Secrets

Our home became a house of secrets and horror. To the outside world, as highlighted in the earlier chapters, we were a normal, perfect family. But inside, the truth was far from what was real. The children grew up in an environment of fear, constantly aware of their father's volatile temper. They learned to stay quiet, to avoid drawing attention to themselves, just as I had. It didn't occur to me that the kids were slowly developing anxiety and PTSD. Despite everything, I tried to maintain some semblance of normalcy for the sake of our children. I wanted them to have a future, to escape the cycle of abuse. I worked hard and saved money for their education, hoping that one day they would be free of the darkness that hung over our home.

Chapter 5: The Inheritance Stolen

As the years passed, I realized that my efforts to save for the children's future were in vain. He had taken control of our finances, giving countless excuses for not being able to provide, using God and religion to hide his laziness. He kept spending my own money and the money I was keeping aside for the children. He was so clever, taking all the family finances. One method he used was maxing out his credit cards frequently. He knew I cannot stand debts so he always used my anxiety as a safety net to clear them off.

It was after I left him did I realized what his system was and made sure to pass the warning to everyone in a relationship to never take it upon themselves to be paying their spouse's debts, especially when you know that that spouse has no regard for family finances. He not only used the credit card methods to take from the family, but also siphoned away every penny meant for the inheritance after we left him.

When I say he's a clever man, he for sure was a clever one in a scrupulous way. During the relationship, I realized that all he does is make excuses for not working hard by saying he cannot stoop so low as to do menial jobs. But when I did it as a woman and brought the money home, he never complained about spending it. As said earlier, when I noticed this, I decided not to give him any physical cash and opted to buy properties for the three children so we can manage it for each of them until they grow up to inherit their individual properties.

Little did I know that he had other plans for his own life. His goal was to take everything and leave nothing behind for the kids, other than a trail of debts and despair. Thus, when we left, he sold all the properties belonging to the kids contrary to the court's instructions and never gave a dime to the children that's meant to inherit the properties.

The betrayal of his actions and his words of being the provider was profound. I had sacrificed so much to ensure our children would have a better future, only to see it all taken away by the man who should have been protecting them. It was another form of abuse, another way to exert his control and keep us all under his thumb.

The properties in question are listed below. To date, my children and I have only received 28.2% of the first house, while he has held on to the remaining properties in their entirety.

Chapter 6: The Unforgivable Sin Happened

The unforgivable sin happened the day he finally killed my firstborn. No one could prepare any mother to see the end of her Son as I saw mine on the fateful day of February 8th, 2016. The day still looks like a bad dream that no mother on this planet would want to dream of. Our Son was found dead in his father's car.

I believed he had finally gotten rid of this amazing young man whom he'd been so envious of for a very long time. The children were already dying from the extensive verbal, physical, and emotional torture they've been receiving from their own father in their own house.

This innocent soul was found dead in a closed garage inside his own dad's car at the age of almost 25. We (The rest of the little ones and I) believed he killed him because that young man had no access to the car key. We asked the so called dad how did boy got hold of his car key, the supposed dad said he forgot the key in the young man's room, mind you, him and the boy haven't been talking for months as the boy lived in the basement far away from the second floor the rest of the family lived on.

The most outrageous acts came from this cold dad by showing no care for the boy found in his car; he did all he could to make sure the paramedics did not have full attention to save the boy. He started banging on the ambulance, calling on the paramedics to help him with his chest pain while they were struggling to save our son. He also took a selfie with our son's corpse while he thought no one was looking, which I don't know how to talk about more.

This despicable human killed our son by making sure he drove him into developing PTSD and depression through constant abuse in the house. Which father beat his own child and sent him out naked into the cold at -27 degrees Celsius? That's one of the countless punishments he gave to this boy while I was thousands of miles away at work. The man who refused and was utterly lazy to work was, at the same time, mistreating the children he was supposed to take care of.

I know my son was driven to depression by this man. I tried all I could to save him, took him to countless counselling but as much as I tried to right the wrong, the father always torpedoed all the efforts to make him better. As soon as we would get home from whichever treatments we went to, he'd start discounting what we went for by demeaning the poor soul, labelling him as lazy (so much coming from a lazy father himself, who never provide for the family), beat him up for little things, smashing his playstation, computers, phones etc.

To cut a long story short, my son was so tired that he moved away from home. I had to go beg him to move back home when I learnt about his situation outside, a decision I regretted up till today.

As soon as he went back, the abuse started all over again. The mystery of how he managed to get into a car without having the keys is something only his so-called father can solve.

Our son was found in his father's car, long gone from Carbon monoxide (CO) poisoning. The circumstances surrounding the tragedy again were shrouded in his lies and deception, but deep down, we knew he was responsible for the son's passing. The loss of our child was a pain beyond words, a wound that would never heal.

In my grief, I felt a rage unlike anything I had ever known. How could someone be so cruel, so devoid of humanity? Yet, I remained in that toxic environment, too broken and afraid to leave, fearing what might happen to the rest of my children if I did. The trauma of losing my innocent child's soul bothers the hell out of me. As my surviving kids and I were going through the grieving process, I noticed this man felt no remorse about the unfortunate circumstances. We found ourselves grieving the loss of the first one in the household. He just went on as if nothing happened, while we were in sorrow, he said he was taking the loss in stride by going on with life as if we just lost a nonliving being.

Chapter 7: The Breaking Point

After we buried our son, months passed in a blur of pain, fear, and survival. I had learned to live in the darkness, to endure the endless cycle of sadness, reliving the pain of losing a child, my first born for that matter. My brain was flooded with cycles of abuse that I and the kids went through with this human.

He maltreated us to the highest extent. The one that passed away bore the biggest brunt of his wickedness with constant traumas of verbal, psychological, and physical abuse and torture. I still can't understand why a father could detest his own children and wife that much. As time went on, we discovered that he had even darker secrets than we ever thought and imagined. It was the death of our Addy that revealed the several lives he had outside the marriage. We discovered he had fathered multiple children with other women over the years, creating secret lives while he destroyed mine.

The realization hit me like a sledgehammer. He wasn't just an abuser; he was a predator, living multiple lives and leaving a trail of broken ones in his wake. It was the final straw, the moment I knew I couldn't continue living in the shadow of his cruelty.

Chapter 8: The Secrets Unveiled**

Armed with the truth, I began to uncover the full extent of his deception. I found letters, texts, pictures, and evidence of some of his other relationships. The man I had lived with for almost thirty years was a stranger, a manipulator who had built his life on lies, a murderer who murdered our son, and an exploiter who exploited everything around him for his benefit alone.

As bad as the situation was with the loss of my son, the situation gave rise to strength I never knew I had. Even though all the revelations of his atrocities of cheating, abusing, killing, and squandering were devastating, it also gave me the strength I needed to start thinking about escape. I could no longer allow myself or my children to be victims of his twisted games anymore. The time had come to break free, to reclaim the life that had been stolen from us.

Chapter 9: Finding Strength in Despair

Breaking free from an abusive relationship is never easy, especially after so many years of being under someone's control. But I found strength in my despair, a resolve to protect my children and give them the life they deserved. I began quietly planning our escape, seeking help from trusted friends and support groups.

I had to be careful; any sign that I was trying to leave could trigger more violence. But the fear of what might happen if I stayed was greater than the fear of leaving. I gathered what little resources I could, knowing that the road ahead would be difficult. I knew it was a path I had to take.

Chapter 10: Breaking Free

The day we finally left was both terrifying and liberating. I took the children and whatever belongings we could carry, and moved to another house, leaving the horror house behind. There were tough moments, fear of how we were going to survive, but the overwhelming sense of relief and freedom kept us going.

Starting over wasn't easy. We had close to nothing as he sold our investment properties even contrary to court orders. But I was glad to leave the scars of years of abuse behind, despite all the emotional and financial hardships ahead. For the first time in decades, we were free from the shadow of his cruelty. It was a new beginning, a chance to rebuild our lives on our own terms.

Chapter 11: Healing and Recovery

The journey to healing was long and filled with challenges. We all had to confront the trauma of the past and learn how to live without the constant fear that had dominated our lives. Therapy, support groups, and the love of those who truly cared for us became our lifelines.

The surviving children, though deeply affected by their experiences and trauma of losing their big brother, began to find their ways in the world. They pursued their education, careers, and personal lives, determined not to let their father's legacy of abuse define their futures. It was a slow process, but with time, we're all beginning to heal.

Chapter 12: Moving Forward

Years have passed since we escaped that dark chapter of our lives. The scars remain, but they no longer define us. We've built new lives, filled with love, support, and a sense of peace that we never thought possible. The children are still struggling, but they are managing better, and I've found strength in my independence.

Looking back, I see the woman who was once trapped, afraid, and hopeless. But I also see the woman I've become strong, resilient, and determined. I survived thirty years of abuse, and though it nearly destroyed me, it also forged a strength I never knew I had.

Lessons Learned

This story isn't just about surviving abuse; it's about finding the strength to rebuild, to reclaim a life that was nearly lost and to appreciate the life that was lost along the journey, making it a life lesson for others coming behind to follow in order not to find themselves in the same spot.

It's also a reminder that even in the darkest of times, there is hope. No one deserves to live in fear, and no one should have to endure what I did.

If you are in a situation like mine, know that you are not alone, and there is a way out. It may be difficult, it may seem impossible, but there is always hope. You are stronger than you think, and you deserve a life free from fear, free from pain, and full of love.

Leaving abusive lives behind will make you discover that you're stronger than you think, and you are better than your abuser. You'll finally be able to realize that those who abuse others are hollow, feckless humans with no backbones, and the evident was proven by our own abuser.

When we left, he went ahead, remarried, and started using bullying tactics, trying to instill more pain by making a mockery of my late son on social media. But at the end of it all, we ignored it all, forged ahead. However, he tried to crawl back to me and the kids, but we know a leopard will never change its spots. So, we never gave him that power of allowing him into our lives anymore, so that the saying once beaten twice shy doesn't apply to our lives.

I Later learned that the new, younger wife he remarried had also passed away. HOW? I have no clue, and I'm not interested in knowing why. All I know is that when my Son died, it was a celebration to him. In fact, I was told that he did have a celebration of life after the younger girl he acquired passed away. And it was after this that he started sending flowers and trying to get back to me and the kids through various avenues. But the lesson had already been learned; marrying and staying with an abusive man for more than 3 decades is enough in this lifetime, and I plan to never get myself mixed up with such a dark soul ever again.

Going through these three tumultuous decades of abuse with the loss of a Son and finances made it impossible to ignore the effects of abuse on those on the receiving end of it. I hope that you're never in the same position, but if you are in one, know that you'll find the strength to face your fears. The purpose of this book is to explore how you can shift your perspectives to regain control and optimism in your life. Learning how to spot a bad partner will give you a hedge against an abusive partner in your life. Therefore, my biggest advise to anyone going into any kind of relationship is to be smart, vigilant, and savvy enough to spot a partner who has traits of abuse. Better to live your life alone and in peace rather than being in an abusive union, and to this, I say, best of luck to couples going into relationships.

Epilogue: Traits of an Abusive Partner & Relationship Advice

Not sure why life threw this kind of melancholy experience on my path, but it for sure gave me the strength and courage to keep living and then be able to help others through this book. It is for sure that life is sweet when you have someone loving, amazing, and truthful to share it with, but my experience definitely gave me an insight into what a better life with a partner is, and thus offered me the opportunity to write this story. I'm here to let you know what you need to accept and reject in a relationship so that you never find yourself in the same position I am today. Therefore, the best advice is never to rush into any relationship. Take your time to know your partner whom you want to spend the rest of your life with, and be careful of anyone who has these 10 traits highlighted below:

Traits of an Abusive partner

1. Controlling Behavior
2. Gaslighting
3. Explosive Temper
4. Blame shifting
5. Love bombing after each abuses
6. Isolating you from friends and families
7. Jealous and Possessive
8. Threats and Intimidation
9. Constant Criticism
10. Disrespect for boundaries

My ex-spouse possessed all of the above traits plus much more and I did avoid all the warnings but eventually paid the big price of bringing innocent children under such an abusive father and the results was the loss of my son and everlasting pain inflicted on me and the siblings left behind, please put it in mind that after noticing most or all of these traits above, that should be a clue that this is not a human to stick around with because at the end of the day, he or she will also cause you misery in the near future as mine did.

It's essential that not everyone is the same, so please never be quick to judge, but do your due diligence before thinking your partner is an abusive human. It's also true that relationship takes work, but sticking around with a man/woman with abusive traits should be never be part of work needed to be done by anyone in any relationship whatsoever but if it is just a little misunderstanding, it is for sure worth the time to salvage that kind of relationships and to that I'll offer my 10 ways to making that relationship work better and making sure you do not fall into the kind of traps I fell into. Though my life as a wife and mother has been filled with ups and downs, I did gain insurmountable experiences through these ordeals, and sharing my story is my way of turning adversity into something educational. If my lifelong struggle helps one couple avoid similar pitfalls, all my pains will be worth it so:

Here are 10 uplifting educational advice for couples to help improve their relationship situation:

Relationship Advice

1. Listen to understand, not to reply. Give your partner your full attention, reflect back what you heard, and confirm you got it right before sharing your own view.

2. Fight the problem, not each other. Frame conflicts as a shared puzzle to solve ("us vs. the issue") rather than a battle to win.

3. Schedule "maintenance" check-ins. Set aside 20–30 minutes weekly to discuss feelings, goals, and any simmering concerns—before they boil over.

4. Show micro-kindness daily:Small gestures, an encouraging text, a cup of coffee, a genuine thank-you compound into big feelings of security and love.

5. Keep curiosity alive:Make sure to ask open questions about dreams, worries, and new interests; people keep evolving, and so should the conversation.

6. Share the mental load: Invisible tasks (planning meals, remembering birthdays, tracking bills) count as real work; divide them consciously and revisit often.

7. Protect couple time: Block out distractions (phones, kids, work) for regular dates or simple rituals like evening walks; consistency matters more than cost.

8. Apologize well: Offer a real apology because a real apology names the hurt, takes responsibility, and offers repair: for example, say, "I'm sorry I snapped; you didn't deserve that. Can we restart?"

9. Celebrate each other's wins: When one partner succeeds, treat it as a joint victory because enthusiastic support builds trust and positivity. Do this by investing in individual growth because Healthy partners make healthy partnerships; pursue hobbies, friendships, and self-care so you bring a full, vibrant self to the relationship.

10. Finally, remember that no matter what, always remember that you and your partner were not brought up in the same household, so the difference might take a while to get used to, so please take your time to make things right.

11. While following all these steps highlighted above, what you should never take, though, is accepting abuse from any human, including your partner. Life is too short to live in an abusive environment, coming from someone that lost a beautiful soul because of ceaseless abuse from his own father, I know first hand that it's not worth living in an abusive environment nor allow any human to destroy your beautiful soul endowed on you by the Almighty God and that concludes the story.

In Loving Tribute to My Dear, Amazing, Gentle Giant Son, Addy.

A beautiful, compassionate, and extraordinarily empathetic soul that was snatched from us too soon.

Son, though you've gone to a better place, your spirit lives on. This story is for you.

I love you, SON.

No matter where you are, honey, Mama loves you.

Your beautiful memories will forever shine within me and in the hearts of your siblings.

-   Adieu, Addy.

www.ingramcontent.com/pod-product-compliance
Lightning Source LLC
Chambersburg PA
CBHW051253120626
46547CB00014B/1920